From Rov

Chris Kinsey

Fair Acre Press

First published in Great Britain in 2019
by Fair Acre Press
www.fairacrepress.co.uk

ISBN 978-1-911048-36-7

Typeset and Cover Design by Nadia Kingsley

Front Cover Image: *Rowan above Abergwesyn Pass* © Sarah Jameson
www.sarahjameson.co.uk

From Rowan Ridge

Mountain Ash

fused onto rock

best tree for

drawing blood from stone.

Previous publications by Chris Kinsey

Kung Fu Lullabies, Ragged Raven Press, 2004
Cure for a Crooked Smile, Ragged Raven Press, 2009
Swarf, Smokestack Books, 2011
Muddy Fox, Rack Press, 2017

Some Responses to Previous Publications

Understated, accurate, fresh, unpretentious language, used to
capture a special moment, making the fleeting magic of it
permanent... She is a true nature poet, attuned to the rhythms of
the wild, glad of the mud, sniffing the darkness.
R.V. Bailey (Envoi)

Chris Kinsey's poems have a kind of earthbound magic.
Sarah Law (Orbis)

Her gaze is sharp, compassionate and wide-ranging, finding
expression through lyrical grace and linguistic invention.
Graham Mort

The metaphors which drive this poetry don't come consciously,
darts aiming for the bull of audience reaction, but from a deeply
internalized source; the impression is that they're fused to the
subject-matter.
Roberta J Dewa (Poetry Nottingham)

This laconic poetry has a voice of its own – a fresh voice. It uses
words as if they have just been invented.
U.A. Fanthorpe

Chris Kinsey may deny that her interactions with the natural world and their expressions in her poetry are anything to do with the spiritual in a traditional sense, but things happen in my atheistic soul when I read her poems that both ground me and send me soaring like the swift.
Zoe Gilbert in Assent Poetry Journal

Kinsey shows a real talent for reading the lives of others with an excitement that infuses the experience with vitality and vicarious joy.
John Ballam Cold Mountain Review

These poems have mapped out a territory of their own, both in form and content.
Carol Rumens

Kinsey's best talent, in my view, lies in seizing speech to reveal character. It's a great thing to be able to do. Shakespeare after all built his reputation on it. It's a skill which permits her to be memorable which is what all poets in the end are after.
Alan Dent Mistress Quickly's Bed

Attunement with nature is experienced as a source of nourishment throughout these poems. Kinsey has a deep knowledge of the flora and fauna of Wales and eye for detail.
Mary Jacob (Planet Magazine)

The poems display a sharp mind at work, her images and stance surprise us, as all good poems should.
There is an appealing humanity in Chris's gaze. Sure, her gaze is crystal but you can have ice and sun in the same mix can't you?
Roz Goddard

Kinsey is at her best with nature. The language is striking.
Rachel Redford (Poetry Review)

Contents

On place

All my life I have had a strong affinity for the rivers and hills of Mid-Wales' borderland. Sometimes I played with other children but, at the age of two, my best friend was the Pinsley stream which flowed past our house and, at that time, on through the centre of Leominster town. Street games with their rules, requirements to conform and domination by older kids weren't as exciting as going exploring upstream.

The stream was a gentler, much more generous, companion which introduced me to a myriad of creatures and plants. I felt a close kinship with nature and seldom wanted to go indoors or into town. I learned to read the river: safe shallows and shingles, the treachery of silt and still deeps.

When I had to start school I suffered terrible separation anxiety. A sand tray and plasticine were poor substitutes for mud and cow pats. It took me a long time to acclimatise to captivity and human-only company. Though I did make friends, I was delighted to get back to the river, the frogs, mayflies and moorhens.

As I grew, Mum became increasingly housebound so I found myself becoming her scout reporting on everything I saw on my explorations. My territory was also her childhood territory. She helped me to identify places to visit, and she created a love of observing and naming birds and wild flowers. Her father took her upstream when he fished the Pinsley and Lugg and I shared his passion for water meadows. My aunt once said to my mother, "Do you think she's our dad come back to us?" I longed to be able to fish like him but no one left in the family had any expertise. Occasionally I was given a brown trout or grayling to cheer Mum up.

My father came from Germany and whenever we visited I got very homesick. That was watery border country too but indistinguishable from Holland: flat and ruled by straight roads, straight trees and dykes. The best bits were playing with my cousins on bomb sites under cover of wild spinach and rose bay willowherb. I craved the hills, meanders, twisting hedges and broken-backed willows of home.

When we were travelling home in 1963, Dad read Beeching's railway cuts aloud from the paper.
The Leominster-to-Kington line that ran past us was to go.
I was 7 and panicked. I thought we'd never get home and I'd have to live in a flat, intensively plotted, place. I pined in anticipation of the loss of wildness and the suffocating weight of sky in the absence of hills.

Even Herefordshire began to feel too low-lying and farmed. Town was encroaching on country. If there was a chance of a rare car trip I always wanted to go west to the Radnor Forest, to Knighton and Presteigne, places imbued with stories of grandfather as a boy staying up all night in Stapleton Castle to stalk its ghost; sometimes we visited grandmother's childhood homes in the hills around Bishops Castle and at the back of the Long Mynd. Topography talked to me. I loved the rounded, unenclosed hills of bilberry and bracken and hiding in secret cwms.

On the way to Barmouth when I was nine, we travelled the

hill road from Knighton to Newtown. I made my uncle stop the car on the moors by Cilfaesty Hill, near the source of the Teme and was enthralled. As we dipped down past the then derelict Cider House, on the back of Kerry hill, at the place I now think of as Rowan Ridge, I spotted a raven leaning into the north and knew, instantly, that I wanted to live nearby.

Chris Kinsey, 2019

Prelude

Swinging high over grown-ups' talk
or sunbathing – front garden bored –
my eyes drift from earwigs pincing gladioli
to the distant scarp of Hay Bluff – the trig point
of all my school bus journeys, bike rides & hikes.
Black Mountains, Brecon Beacons, Radnorshire Hills,
lured me from the lowlands to their crinkled horizons
promising the source of streams, mawnpools, cwms,
with common land, ravens & wild ponies.

Family Flowers

Out along the hedgerow
after the memorial ceremony
Everyman's flowers flourish uncut.
Forget-me-nots and alkanets out-blue
the sky washed clear by early storms.
Buttercups dish up sunshine – lighting
the tunnel of sycamore, oak and maple.
You picked buttercups for a tune
which stopped time. Polka notes
airing the church set me back a century
picturing my grandparents stepping out
of their wedding vows to dance
down the aisle in muslin and lace.
Out here, cow parsley sheds white,
elderflowers strain and tang the light
and stitchwort prints the sward
with stars fallen from whitening nights.
Deep amongst campions and herb robert,
fox moths cast off cocoons to frenzy
the flowers, drunk on pheromones and nectar.
I think of you dancing and composing the airs
of these lanes and consider my aunt
as a girl on the back of this mynd.
So in thrall to wild flowers, she waded

2. Frog Juniors

So much for *Hopscotch, Tiddleywinks* and tame T.V.
– for staying indoors and doing as told.

She sets off on safaris and finds ponds
with eyes like lost property.

Every day she stares the spawn specks wide
'til winking, wiggling, they shuck their jelly.

She learns *Tadpole* and wonders if they're
called it for squirming on top of their spheres.

Big heads, whip bodies, they thrash out legs
– Summer of *Twist & Shout, Rock & Roll*

She can't hear them *Shout* but they sure do
Twist in Metamorphosis.

Frogs teach her to hop, bop, chuckle and mime.
She gets detention for *leapfrogging* the P.E. queue.

3. A-Level Frog

Spawn pilgrimages stopped when she started her teens.
Her next frog came vacuum-packed from the refrigerator.

Teachers counselled against mixing science with literature
Perhaps it would have stopped the dissonance –

going straight from a single lesson of Wordsworth
to double Biology, quoting:

Our meddling intellect
Mis-shapes the beauteous forms of things
We murder to dissect.

She takes the delicately fingered manus and flippered
kick limbs and pins them to the altar of board

picks up the surgical scissors, and, gulping, pinches
the loose skin near the cloaca, snips and cuts a median line

guided by the sternum. She tailors some transverse cuts
to ease the skin back, pins it like a tail coat and gasps

expecting a road-kill spill of guts but everything's intact
fibres and cavities hold; all's layered neat as a relief map:

muscle topography, strata of bone, navigate arterial roads,
venous lanes – scalpel and expose, expose –

trophy the gallbladder from lobes of liver like a cocktail caper,
practice tying off blood vessels. Her teacher's in raptures:

Such precise little hands!
The *straight A* boys tsk, glower and nip off all the wrong bits.

Week 4, they're down to the nerves,
teasing the long white sciatic kick.

Forget *air guitar* – she and the only other arts-science boy
mime *Duelling Banjos* – a bit of finger-picking bad faith –

twanging future aches.

Black Mountain Chapel

In the hill country at the moor's edge
There is a chapel, religion's outpost
In the untamed land west of the valleys ~ R. S. Thomas

This stone room in the hill's roll
shuts the door on ewe cries
and spats between buzzard and crow.
It offered more than the ministries
of wind, rain and limping sheep.

Hard to know how they felt,
the people who worshipped here in 1850.
I doubt they saw the elevation
as taking them closer to heaven –
easy living is sacrificed on altitude's altar.

Did the pulpit arouse preaching fervour?
Stern words to strengthen hardy people
with hopes of improvement?
Twin windows draw my eyes west
I doubt the faithful ever saw it this green.

Cwm Eicen's brush of tawny rushes
points to a time when every field
had its font and quota of curlew
and snipe. Brown hares couldn't jink
engines of drainage and re-seeding.

The congregation knew the properties
of lime, worked hard to see off birch,
hawthorn, gorse and bracken.
Subsidies' uniform Eden
and sighing conifer plantations

might seem prayers answered.
Successors recede with the flushes –
over-cropped sorrel, tormentil and thyme.
Presence lingers in silence
in the absence of skylarks and curlews.

Eden was a vacant lot

'Come away, O human child!
To the waters and the wild' ~ W.B. Yeats

Her getaway is the red pedal car.
It's hard to drive on the unmade road
so she parks on the vacant lot.

Small weeds welcome her:
Knotgrass, scarlet pimpernel
and a wealth of shepherd's purses.

Who wants to nap when there's bitter
dandelions to milk and chamomile
hearts to pinch and sniff?

Willowherb and goldenrod wave
her in Grand Prix style, conspiring
to hide her and keep all secrets.

A violet ground beetle guides her to
the cracks and kiting spiders spin
safety lines for her solo acts.

Cinnabar and burnet moths, daytime's
poison beauties, swirl spots before her eyes
and flash scarlet-black stripes.

she watches goldfinches charm
thistle crowns. Down flies – someone
tells her airborne seeds are fairies

Make a wish! Make a wish!

Call the Greyhounds:

Dew-dancer
Wind-racer
Blade-bracer

Thicket-striker
Cloud-galloper
Lightning-bones

Heart-thunderer
Shadow-lancer
Cat-setter

Squirrel-chaser
Deer-heeler
Hare-acer

Sprung-spine-springer
Tumble-teaser
Puddle-leaper

Pool-cooler
Quilt-snuggler
Dream-twitcher

Hearth-gracer

Four visits to Mitchell's Fold.

1. *May 2010*

This stone circle sheathed Excalibur,
caught the witch who milked
the magic cow into a sieve;
held back trickery, greed,
mischief, famine.

These petrifying stones,
shunted and plundered,
trap scraps of the sacred,
hold stories. We huddle
to sense what remains.

The lark strikes –
soaring on song past
the circling peregrine.
Shrug off history, myth, feel winter's
hard dry bite on over-grazed grass.

Bracken is slow to fiddle cattle
to this high summer pasture
shelved between countries
tipped between times where
paths and sightlines scramble;

traipsed by axe-traders,
farmers, miners, trippers.

2. *April 2011*

The standing stones have shrunk,
sunk deeper into dry earth.

Off west – raven hustles peregrine –
some nonchalant flicks, a few

controlled tumbles and they settle
to contest the crags in silent stand-off.

Along the saddleback to Stapeley Hill,
lark song lights grates of scorched gorse.

A leashed hound on the skyline strains
to bound down to our two.

Wild Edric's dogs thundered here.
Now three unbound commoner's beasts,

coursing under curlew's cries,
would make a wild hunt.

3. *Royal Wedding 2011*

Haze dissolves horizons;
along the common, larks sing themselves invisible;
four lapwings abracadabra eggs, decoying nests

scraped into brittle grass and dry lichen.
The last Lancaster Bomber drones over
fluttering the wild heartsease.

East of the Cow stone, under the summit,
a cow circle chews, heartbeats race –
fear that flickering hound-shadows will start a stampede.

We hurry back to the fold through hollows
screened by last year's bracken,
tracing the footsteps of axe-traders, farmers, miners;

shelved between countries,
tipped between times
in the scramble of now.

4. *July 2016*

The stones bite through a beard of bracken.
Grazing sheep keep the circle shaved
but for wavy hair-grass stippling
heath speedwell and tormentil.

A short stand back, foxgloves rocket,
lark notes cascade over bedstraws' stars.

Dipping into the cwm my ears strain
to make it an amphitheatre for curlews.
There's a hesitant *cur-lee, cur-lee* –
real cry, or mimicry?

A bouquet from Clun Castle

Peals of bluest harebells.
Trefoils, bedstraws, thistles.
Red grasses roan with morning rain.
The season's first heather patch.
White yarrow, pink yarrow
and one yarrow a scarlet ladybird camp.
Hedge woundwort, marsh woundwort
betony, purple loosestrife, mallow
and the top digits of foxgloves.

*

Swallows scythe the bailey
Martins shoot from the tower
as a Sparrowhawk erases
himself on grey cloud.

At the sign saying
This was a 14C hunting preserve
my greyhounds give me the slip.

Invigilating a Maths Exam

We start with a sigh
and the bickering of blackbirds.
Scratchy biro, calculator tap, tap.
One blackbird sings out in triumph.
Pencil scribbles – then line obeys rule.
A wren trills in rivalry.
Heavy hatching and scoring –
art covering over not-knowing.
Thump of feet despite being cased
in Nike Air. Crows dispute chip papers.
The train rumbles through on time.
Synchronised gulps of water.
By the time we finish, the leaves
on the graveyard elder have opened.

Busker

"The future has an ancient heart." ~ Carlo Levi

He's not from round here – the musician
talking with his violin, conjuring more than he knows,
setting sounds to flight, soaring over peaks

ravines, forests and steppes. He plays the dance
of the Northern Lights beyond a shtetl,
rouses howling winds, whining dogs, sobbing gulls.

Strings mimic ice floes, lapping water – flights
of migrating swans seeking winter refuge. His violin knows
the weightlessness of fugitives crossing borders.

Fingered notes call and respond, lost – found, lost – found.
They draw men from the dark corners of a bar
exile others from a betting shop's bright screens

out to the street where afternoon's already turned night.
Under town lights his violin's the colour of a good harvest.
Ripe notes scatter. The musician with the faraway look

cocks his head expecting birds to come pecking
out of spring forests. He waits for one to land by his ear
and start singing duets to his trills.

A charm of goldfinches

scatter over roadside dandelions.

Gorse-bright,
a prick of blood behind the beak,
they steal blowing silver

and spin it from down
to gold filaments.

A nod to William Carlos Williams

So little depends
upon

an aluminium wheel
barrow

reclining
on the compost heap

yellow wheel
rinsed with rain

beneath gold
finches singing

up dandelions.

Mute

The only cloud

    in the flood's new sky

        is a lone swan

grazing rushes

    unperturbed

        by train clatter

or its ghost partner's

    rising reflection.

Watching for Season Change

So much starts in the dark
slowly, without signalling –
tiny alignments, adjustments
like the stretch of root caps
tapping softening soils,
sap gathering. Chickweed,
sheltered in pavement cracks,
is already tender-leaved,
blooming with hailstones.

Preparing for spring
is like squaring up
to a martial arts master –
watching for deep stirrings,
spotting first moves.
I'm steady, in no great rush
to get out of winter.
I like ice sunrises
and the stripped forms of trees.

Dread unbalances me –
first swallow late to Abbeyfield wires
arums slow in arrowing verges
signify sharp decline,
creatures lured out of hibernation
too soon will starve
and frogs, newts and toads
will turn into road-kill
or find their spawning pool dry.

Delight unsettles too:
the suddenness of celandines
to strike a light to dead hedges,
primroses speed in
pastelling old brambles.
When fresh grass spears
turn my greyhounds to grazing gazelles
and the great cherry races start,
I submit.

The surge depends
on a tuning to light, a certain warmth.
If climate shifts
out of calling range
we will all lose our footing.

February on Reservoir Hill

Anthills are sealed against frost and wind.
The moon has slipped tethers of brown grass
and rises early through cloudless blue.

A bullfinch flushes the hawthorn gap
but his mate whistles him back to the south slope
where buds will open first.

Down in the housing estate a starling ruffles
up sunset and churrs into the north wind
seeking the rest of its roost-bound flock.

Roadside Lurcher

3.00 a.m. we're out washed in moonlight
with the wan tendrils of dead nasturtiums.
The vet's opiate hasn't brought any ease
and you pace your pain from plant to plant.

Snowdrop buds bead dark soil like coils
of dropped rosaries – so late this year
I've felt their absence many times
now they're conspicuous in starlight.

Their silent keeping of white light soothes me
but not you. Each one's a dice dot which shakes
you blundering a new direction, crying softly.
The owl, haloed in the tree, hears you.

January's no time to be out long in pyjamas
So we camp by the stove and shake together.
Arched high under my fingers your tremors diminish,
but you're tense as the day you were rescued.

The First Time Firecrests Cross My Path

A whir
     Two spheres,
            smaller than pine cones,
drop
     through the tree's needles.
Wings blur
      brushing snow
         from the last branch.
Cock circles hen
      in a loop,
        loop,
         loop-chase.
Courtship
     or gnat-dance?

The brand of his crest
      burns off fog

hers dips and lights
      January groundsel.

Mild January

The blackbird ransacking moss
is turning over the old year.
Each dusk he digs up a little more light
to delay evening's ructions.
This morning dammed light spills over the hill –
four fields stitched by a low rainbow.
Down here, at the end of it, earthworms
invent copulation – so raw in their slip
of mucilage and eggs – worth more
than gold to the bird casting nearby.
His eye and bill ring the daffodils
spreading alarm by flowering before
snowdrops have priested frost.

Last train from Aberystwyth

'Don't mind my bag, love.
Go on, sit down.
I'll sit yer, by the aisle –
Got long legs, see.
You know what they say –
The higher they are,
The harder they fall.'

He sways, starts yodelling,
'T – i-i-m- B- e-rrr'
and crashes diagonally across
the gangway and opposite seats.

'Sometimes this leg just collapses on me –
poor circulation from sleeping rough.
You got no idea where I been.
Been in a very bad place
but believe me; I'm doing my utmost to get out of it.
Got the old man on at me for showing no remorse.
I told him, 'It's the time of year.
It's the wrong time of year for remorse.'

I got beat up New Year,
That's what I'm doing with this shiner.

I live on the streets or on the trains if I can afford it.
What's the fare to Borth, Mitch?'
Mitch twitches to music, his eyes
are well into the last phases of the moon.
'How much is the fare –?

I don't wanna get put off –
I been put off some hellish places –
Craven Arms. That place is THE END.
Welshpool, that's a hard old place.
Was even put off in Dyfi Junction once.
But that night I had Hayley with me.'
The name penetrates Mitch's song.
"What, Hayley that makes the disgusting films?"
'Yeah, disgusting films.'

The train lurches into Borth. Mitch pulls the plugs.
Paranoid thrashes the carriage:
"Black Sabbath, Led Zeppelin, Deep Purple.
Remember 'em? Your era aren't they?"
Heavy metal charges them out.
Deep Purple starts in my skull:
Black night, black night
I can't see dark light
Maybe I'll find on the way the line
That I'm free...
Black night is a l-o-n-g way from h-o-o-me.

As we hurtle darkness into Dyfi Junction
the chorus howls, guitar gods fade.
Under the empty ospreys' nest,
I picture footprints,
a reed-bed swaying,
two new creeks in the saltmarsh ...
Skinner and Hayley streamed live
on webcam.

Biohazard

From a distance a new dune rises
behind the line of driftwood and dreck.
Dumped by sifting tides, a dead minke
lies on the estuary's southern spit.
Black and yellow biohazard signs
are anti-invitations to go and gawp.
We go close in, stare at rarity,
try to fathom this beached limousine
of the deep. We get caught in its
cause-of-death-mystery: poison,
netting, led astray by the siren-song
of manmade sonar?

Does the creature care
now that its flukes are frayed
and it is headfirst into decomposition -
baleen plates beaking from a lost face?
All the dragged-along-dogs look away
united in uninterest for something too big,
too strange to comprehend. Perhaps,
sensing the swell of gases, they fear
she'll blow? We stand the shocks
of harpoons still wounding whales,
pounding their huge hearts, killed
for the bounty of their bulk.

Common Salt

Tenth Christmas I dismissed Santa
and was thrilled – a chemistry set
and microscope matched my wishes.

Casting iron filings and magnet aside
I purpled colourless days with gallons
of potassium permanganate

hoarded the small tube
of heavenly blue copper sulphate
helplessly watching it fade to dull white.

I tilted the microscope mirror furiously
failing to find focus –
suddenly light startled the lens

salt grains clicked into cubes
sharp prisms flaring white light
into rainbows.

Licking spill from my palm
I tasted tears.

Private Collection

I could spell and I could read –
nothing else I knew counted at school.
I failed sums, sequencing and all
the hypotheticals of 11+ reasoning –
more interested in Ivy-leaved toadflax
growing in walls and nits hatching
in Sandra Davies' hair than how much
change a boy would get from buying
three imaginary cakes with a shilling.
Mr Seager, headmaster, sent for me.
Flooded with fear, I racked my brains
for what I'd done wrong. He opened
a Bible, asked me to read The Creation
whilst his secretary totted registers.
He asked me back again and again
to practise passages for assembly.
I grew fluent and curious – longed
to look in his cabinet of thin drawers.

He drew the top one – I rapidly named
all the hot butterflies I'd ever chased:
red admiral, peacock, tortoiseshell,
painted lady, brimstone, comma and
cool cabbage white with wings blotted
like the centre pages of my books.
All with wings flat, easy to I.D. as I-Spy.
Next week it was browns: gatekeepers
skippers, coppers, ringlets, heaths.

Third week, I gasped over elusive blues'
sapphire-violet shimmer. *'And finally,*
my special treasure, caught when cycling
by the Norfolk Broads – a Swallow-Tail…'
I saw the boy emerge from the man. Tiers
of trapped wings landed us on common ground
so I asked, *"Why isn't there Nature in the 11+?"*
He shrugged. *'Keep going for bike rides.'*
I spun to a new school fluttering with ambition.

Winter Jasmine

'We will have Winter Jasmine...'
Mum's words enchant. My two year old mind
instantly set a thicket around our new house.

Mum was never well enough to plant jasmine
but birds dropped scarlet berries and started
cotoneaster bushes blazing to our porch.

Now, in my own garden, sprigs of jasmine
push through berries to bloom by the door
fragile flowers, often teary with too much rain

or glazed with ice, lure me to linger in winter light.
Sun's keepsakes, they star the days before Solstice
daring snowdrops to rise and catkins to cascade.

Back from the end of the line

Tonight I'm on the run from narratives.
I want this near ghost train to run blank film
and wipe my head clear.
Empty seats double, giving night a wide berth.
Lights project fluorescent ribs on to black
a pin-hole moon shines through shuttering.

The only stars to pierce November clouds are hill farms
as we ratchet in stop-frames up to Talerddig Halt,
I don't want complications, arcs or crises,
just want to be rock and rolled home
through what passes for linearity in this folded,
impossible-to-level landscape.

Confession

You can put this down in your book.
We were walking to school, nobody with us.
We just got carried away...

It was a snowy morning – snow all over the fields –
and down by the old lay-by there was a heron.
You don't see one very often, do you?

And when you do – whischt – he's off silent as snowfall.
One of these friends of mine started throwing snowballs.
All four of us threw snowballs...

I think there was something wrong with this one –
I don't think it could fly. Normally they flap and glide.
We didn't mean to... But this one didn't move.

It died. That's true. That's the gospel. Put it down.
I remember it very well. We had three strokes
of the cane and a man from the RSPB came.

Now, whenever I see a heron...

'The Cowshed'

Last night I had a bath with Chagall
and gazed at the cow poking her head
through a shed roof into the violet night.

She is the cow who jumped over the moon
and swallowed it. Swollen in her stall
she glows with celestial grazing.

She knows her importance to the family
behind fiery windows. Breath and steam
condense milky-blue from indigo.

Beyond roof trees the sky is starless.

Cut

Because, like the cat, you were put out whether you wanted to go or not, you started running. Running not like an athlete pushing his personal best but running first from ghosts, the ghosts of the old Gallows Tree. You give shades the slip down cinder paths but their scuffs still drag behind you along the towpath. Under the belly of the bridge, you snatch your breath back from the condemned. Bubbles belch. Drowned things bob amongst lily pads. Brickwork's drip, drip, drip is more urgent than the tick of the kitchen clock telling you you're late for school. You run on empty, dodging down alleyways to the smooth caress of the skatepark's concrete curves and dream of an easy glide. There'll be trouble if you don't get to class.

Tethered to a desk your thoughts rise from books and hover over lesson chants like the fumes of broken nights. The fug of toking strangers twitches and swirls in your living room. They party nights away. In the morning it's a morgue, a Frankenstein's parlour of groaning – cave mouths, eyes that slide too sly to focus. A teacher threatens you with the 'real world'. How much more real than midnight flits across town – hiding from the police in someone else's back bedroom with mum's bottle of whisky as sentry and a baby no one wants to wake?

You don't want to go back. Don't look. Dump your bag through the front door and get off out again. Running, running, nicking chocolate bars the way mum's friend showed you using some stagy sleight of putting a bar back for CCTV and flee. You learn to tend your own wounds – the kerb-kiss split lip – the stone that nearly took your eye. Blood that made a Brownie blanch as you peered for your reflection in the Youth Club's strip-lit glass. She opened the window and urged you in to wash. *You've got blood dripping off your chin.*

Home. Grounded. You man up, hackle your forearm with a cross-hatch of fine red hairs; roll your bones radius to ulna. When the muscles ripple and swell you cut more, make a pelt of scars and go out again. The farmer chases you down Gallows Bank, his scarecrow grin tied to his quad bike by a scarf. Revs roar and you catapult on fence wire then catch on barbs. He's only come to warn you off the ice on the boggy bottom field. *Yesterday a girl fell through and got stuck.* You feel the slice of ice, blind as bathroom window panes, shattering around your shins as you trudge over the blond tussocks that poke through like severed heads.
You say, *I know, I was the one who carried her home.*

They Call Me Red

I don't see it myself.
I wear the same beige Museums' Service uniform as
                                    everyone else.
Friends say I was dipped in Socialism instead of baptised.

The only immersion I've known is the heater
in the airing cupboard and hot water in my bath.
After the Pithead showers – a soak in the bath's a luxury.

Our mam was grateful to the NCB for installing showers
and for washing our filthy overalls.
She remembered her mam, hands red-raw, washing sooty
                                                clouts.

Every Monday washday, she recited:

What is this life if, full of care,
We have no time to stand and stare.
No time to stand beneath the boughs
And stare as long as sheep or cows.

It used to wind the old man up
when he was slogging his guts out down the pit.
In the 1970s, I left school and went with him.

Job for life – I thought.
Had a string of jobs after the mines closed
all of them crap pay and no camaraderie.

When I was out of work I went back to college
history, literature, art appreciation –
all things girls were good at at school.

I think of mam every time I come on shift.
She'd never dreamt that one of hers
would spend his life standing staring.

Becoming Snowbound

Day greys to dusk as more snow slants in.
Before logging-on I thank the bare-knuckled
engineer kneeling at the street cabinet
connecting copper wires D-side to E-side
through blizzard to keep lines open.

I've been shuffling poems west to east
with a friend already snowbound in Norfolk
and read the drifting flakes as her gift
of quietness and retreat.

She sends, *There's a snipe in our garden –*
it has made a cave in the snow
and gets very aggressive
if I go anywhere near.

I picture the bird exposed on snow's fresh page
its oak gall and Indian ink lines conspicuous
not cryptic in marsh reeds and rushes.
No one would earn the name Sniper hunting
this bird flushed from the wisp and starving.

On The New Mining Sculpture Erected In Wrexham Town Centre

"gather me/ Into the artifice of eternity." ~ W.B. Yeats.

I stand alone, stripped to sinew and bone,
icon of the many now dead or redundant.
We were a work force once, waging muscle
and metal against mineral, hewing the coal
that fired steel's furnaces and hissed engines'
multiple revolutions, inspired design.
.

I am a monument to Modernity – my airy
superstructure embodies elements
of the work I defend: earth, air, fire,
carbon, iron and quenching water.
Braced in concrete, fused at pelvis, elbow, knee,
my high-tensile joints never tire.

Cast in combustion, I rise to rally memories
of Gresford's dead. My raised pickaxe scrapes
a bluer sky, stirs old fights for wealth and safety.
A cleaner wind keens for lost camaraderie –
pit and plant sold out in a global exchange.
Hush, there are whispers of regeneration.

False Orchids

My first 999 call –
'Stay with me on the line.'
Fractured talk keeps me from flapping
until, *'I'm sorry, I've got to leave you for another caller.'*

I stare at the false eyes of basking peacocks.
A moment's dead line – no sirens –
whirling blue lights swirl morning round.
Butterflies on the buddleia scatter shadows.

Electrodes stick to a chest that heaves a bucking heart
monitoring discord: Beeps. Cheeps. Shrieks –
misfiring beats shrill and acquire a line.
Klee's notion of taking a line for a walk runs crazy.

This line isn't walking it's hurdling, canyoning.
I'd prefer a slow thud Country beat,
slower than Johnny Cash's freight train snare on
I walk the line, something in 3:42 time.

We're bound straight for Resusc. I sit tight –
try to shut off from screen chaos and cacophony,
cultivate numb endurance, co-operate with answers
to the second medical questionnaire.

He's stretchered off. I'm sent to wait in A & E –
'A paramedic will fetch you shortly.'
I sit with three people hunching dislocations
and a low-volume re-run of mumbling Columbo.

The paramedics don't come.

At Newbridge-on-Wye School

All summer's fires are stoked for Michaelmas.
Temperatures rise: maple, birch and beech blaze.
Out of class, we hunt the words that form
with things and fall: acorns, conkers,
beech nuts spat from empty masts,
casings 'like *velcro*', linings *'like rat fur'*;
words which trace things that vanish
like dew and toadstools; and words that stick,
resin from wafers of silver fir cones.
One boy plucks a shred from air and names
the Sumach *'lava-leaf.'*
A posse of girls take my arm,
"Miss, Miss, come and see the butterfly tree."
The tall flowers, giddy with flame wings
and fluttering shadows, are tousle-headed
michaelmas daisies. Their golden eyes lure:
tortoiseshells, admirals and peacocks
winking back with false eyes, as if
they've been waiting all summer
to hatch into heat and late nectar.

At the Pass (Bwlch Glynmynydd)

You'd open the car door to the inrush of wet bracken,
breathe dilute sheep musk and wait –
This lay-by at the watershed was your limit.

Always your scout, I set off up the track.
I failed to catch your favourite trout but brought back
blackberries, hazelnuts, backpacks of windfalls.

We sat for ages tracking my sightings in books.
This buzzard – almost extinct in your day – would thrill you,
coiling such depth of blue with constant calling.

A hilltop like this, after rain, sometimes studs with mushrooms,
sudden as flying saucers.
I once picked so many that riding my bike home was a circus act.

That night we chopped and fried for the whole street
passing plates trickling with dark buttery juice over fences
getting them back wiped white with bread and butter.

Peeling their soft skins now, sets my fingers remembering
the kid gloves you sewed, home-working. Night after night
I fell asleep to the race of your *Dents'* treadle.

Today, everything in this rare light triples shades.
Flickers over fading heathers trace to red admirals.
Their shadow-play fans my memories of you.

No Going Back

Poppies blazed from cracks by the prefabs
I tugged one – it lashed my palm
snapped with a whiff of underworld.

I cried when the petals fell like bits of burst
balloon. It was the third day
and I didn't want to go to school again.

I wanted to go back to the river
put my hands up and surrender
to brown meadow grasses taller than I was.

Silk Roads

Spiders showed her the ropes –
without them she might have refused school.
She prowled along pavements – only her face
could feel ghost silks. Her four-year-old fingertips
touched and tapped: doubt, doubt, doubt.

She tongued her way down alleys,
found that gossamer had less savour
than stray hair and dandelion down.
Where did the threads come from?
Why weren't they there at home time?

What snared strained and snapped?
Her cheeks felt the physics of curiosity
eyelashes brushing breaking point. Dew made
orbs apparent, mystery condensed, then rime.
She squandered crystal fortunes to enchantment.

Stuck on sums, she stared at cobwebs crazing
the window pane and saw the spider spin
her draglines, droplines, guidelines
and regretted all her breaches of web.
She learned to limber under silk tightropes.

A tremble of tensions triggers spider to abseil,
swathe the trapped housefly with gauze.
It's now just a barrel to tap over days.
Every time it's sums she watches spiders drift
and wonders, if she were better at handstands,

would she develop spinnerets like a money spider?
She wants to cast a thread to the wind and kite free
of classroom captivity. Sometimes she's sent for
and catches the spider holding Class 7 hostage.
She sets it on toadflax – takes the long way back.

The Meteorite Hunters

I just want to get my hands on the rocks,
and hold drops of lemony desert glass,
to finger the force of flash fusion.

Elemental thrills – I'm eager to divine blast
feeling fragments from Heaven's arsenal –
rare metals metamorphosed by ignition.

The guide's soundtrack grows more sensational –
The next shooting star *Could take out civilisation.*
Return to the Dark Ages. Apocalyptic astronomy.

We savour the threat of *extinction*, catch breath
for superhero talk of spotting the signs, doing the sums
and saving the planet from *sterilisation*.

Big guns cue Milton: "Who durst defy th' Omnipotent to arms."
Other plans sound more Tai Chi – cosmic ward-offs
to shift trajectories to glancing fly-bys.

After the tour of the telescope turret we crowd
a small window and orientate ourselves by pointing
at familiar old volcanoes: Brown Clee and tilting Titterstone.

If we're struck now, here, on the cusp of Stonewall Hill,
the world would sigh with relief – another lucky escape,
another hit in a poorly populated place.

There were eye-witnesses in the Amazon to see
The Sun touch the earth. Skin-witnesses in Siberia in 1908:
The sky split in two. It was so hot I wanted to tear my shirt.

I couldn't bear it. But then the sky shut tight and
a strong bang sounded. Like a cannon I was thrown
as a hot wind raced between houses.

We'd be newsworthy for a little longer than
the shockwave, set in statistics and You-Tubed
like Chelyabinsk by dashboard cameras.

Dear Earthwrecked Foundling,

It's the season of second flowerings
so let's go out and play.

Wales is good for sampling light.
We can splash in puddles,
shake up fallen clouds and sludge.

I'll introduce you to birds

Maybe we'll see a kingfisher streak turquoise
over turbulent waters, watch wagtails waver
then settle and learn stillness from a heron.

Now is a good time to meet trees

You can build a refuge of fallen leaves
but don't be alarmed by bombardments of acorns
and conkers. You can forgive them for their shine.

I'll try not to shiver you with my worries -

worries the air will soon be exhausted
soils will fail to raise harvests
fish will suffocate in ocean plastic.

Learn to be surprised now and for the rest of your life.

Today a boy who tossed his school desk like a ship in a tempest
turned up in my yard to choreograph scaffolding poles.
He effortlessly constructed a lattice of planks strong
                                          enough
                                                 to stand on.

I'm surprised

              by you showing up
                      just as all my praise songs

turn to elegies.

Working Museum

At the End of the Day

there's a meeting of muscles.
The horse has shed his harness
and the man sits astride him, easy,
without saddle, holding the reins loosely,
urging him gently to take a little freedom.
Collarless, unblinkered, the Shire almost trots.

Released from the rule of furrow and cart drag,
his muscles make a looser sine wave
still collected, not exuberant.
He follows the prick of his ears
through the parkland that keeps him
in the bowl of labour and production.

I imagine the pair going to pasture
but they return to the loosebox for hay.
How much language of pressures and touch do I retain?
Days when I'd double back from school friends
to a secret orchard, vault onto someone else's pony
and ride without tack like the Gypsies showed me –

clasping a tuft of mane, shifting weight to set direction.
The trick was to trust the thrust, merge with
horsepower and let a gallop beat
the humiliations of Hymn Practice, Needlework,
and the miscalculations of Maths into a dream of riding
away, off timetable, over the hill, into the Wild West.

First Aid

All morning in a windowless room
learning to stem the trickiness of bleeds
rolling healthy strangers into the recovery position
thumping compressions into a dummy with no vital signs.

Lunchtime, I wipe the sting of antiseptic from my lips
go out to clear my airway with a draught of deep September.

Jet vapours unravel like bandages
though the sky over rowans is cloudless.
These scarlet trees have spread their protection
from lone hill-steads to town's corrugated factories.

I pick a sprig to ward off afternoon's harm, carry
a cluster of summer scorch back to artificial light.

River incident

Rain all night;
            house-clearing all day.
Out at last.

The river speaks differently,
            more slap, less chortle
no silent passassages.

A young heron bars the path
stabbing rinds of white bread
and burger cases.

Hold the hounds back
            to avoid a scavenge show-down.
The heron becomes a carnyx

blaring upstream.
Ducks corkscrew in the current,
            all a-clamour and a-quack.

A kingfisher breaks from brown waters,
bagatelles between banks of balsam
and vanishes with its fish.

            Everything is brighter.
Home through showers of goldfinches
winnowing thistledown.

At Cors Caron / Tregaron Bog

Late August afternoon – summer holds its breath.
This bog, rising since the Ice Age, is a cauldron bubbling
the magic span of spells.

Sky tints the peat pools fountain-pen blue
and deeper down where rush quills root
water is the colour of old inkwells.

Quick-shuffling sharp light / strong shade tricks
my eyes back to a time of detentions for *carelessness*
– ink devils blotted my lines.

I longed to be out looking for reptiles, hunted for them
hopelessly in cool cow meadows and down
the columns of a hand-me-down encyclopaedia.

Bible-weighty and certain it challenged:
The title 'common' prefixing lizard is largely a misnomer.
It is unlikely you will be quick enough to see one.

Now, with eyes old enough to flicker motes and doubts,
black shapes skittering off the boardwalk brings unease.
Nothing disturbs the mire, and then I see, in low relief,

dark amulets, marked with dots and dashes,
scrawling over margins. Thrilled, after fifty years,
by this surprise of lizards flouting small-print certainty.

Yews in a Welsh Border Churchyard

Corralled as cattle poisoners
and planted in the mouths of the dead
for immortality
                  these trees were once a royal arsenal.

Now bony roots heave up the recent dead;
           crack the paths of the shaky living.
Dark branches sweep shades off flaking stones
               and scatter blood berries from unseen flowers.

The spirits of Lear's riotous soldiers
        whisper to skilled bowyers:
    Season the staves, bond red heartwood to white sapwood.

Starved of vigour these corpse-fed trees
crave archers to brace their bows –
men with sinews taut enough to set arrows whistling
                 and unsettle old scores.

Another Church Tour

I'm not here out of habit or curiosity
I've filed in with a flock out of politeness
and sit in the stalls feeling shifty.

I want to escape this scripted space:
stained glass stories of suffering, angels'
innocence, kneelers' fading symbols.

Nose tingling on mildewed devotion
I wonder if, just for mischief, I could
switch a hymn number to 666?

Today a historian, not minister,
holds the lectern – building funds supplied
by the rich to save their souls.

Vaulted chapels glorify the gentry
but time's snubbed their effigies
and left them nose-less as lepers.

I'm not made for the monumental,
physics not metaphysics catches my awe:
the might of masons, labourers who cut stone

and hewed timber, respect for engineers
who understand earthly stresses
and how to make them hold.

Comes to Eisteddfa Gurig

d night for a come-back –

Step out under sky's dark coif,
wear blue suede shoes, your moon-white suit.
There's crystals in the frost and quartz,
a sparkle in the stars.

No need for stage fright up here.
The wind has turned its volume way down low.
Mountain grass is too tangled to make bootleg recordings.
Sing the salmon upstream.

Elvis is an anagram for lives.
Manifest for whoever paints your name
on this roadside rock – coat after coat,
for fifty years.

You hit it big, the year I was born:
Heartbreak Hotel, Hound-dog,
But I can't say *You were Always on My Mind*,
only when Valerie, next door, opened her windows.

Prelude to a Tachycardia

Breakfast time I have an outburst
about the vociferousness of machines.
I'm okay with the fridge's old growl-purr
but not the microwave's repeating pterodactyl shrieks
the *instant* 'END' flashes.

I hate the misdialled ring tone of new washing machines.
Especially the one at work where a 'duty of care'
sets me scanning smoke detectors, panicking at the alarm
until I swoop in anticlimax on Gary's boxer shorts
completing their cycle.

I curse the impatience of appliances; all jingle-burble.
Even the recharger's chick-chirrup vexes
striking electronic kinship with my neighbour's
over-eager car locks.
I urge the phone not to ring.

It's August the silent month when song birds give up
defending territory and hideaway to moult,
though quill-throb doesn't stop gulls skewering
hot nights with their randy cruise-cries.
Out in the garden the last warbler fades.

All's not well with the patient in the lawn chair –
my prescription for rest and quiet isn't working –
his runaway pulse races silently.

High Summer on a Shropshire Hill

Cocksfoot, crested dog's tail, Yorkshire fog,
Common bent, Brown bent, Italian rye grass –
sown way back, to improve the ley. Wavy hair-grass,
fine fescues, soft rushes, bromes whose awns irritate
animal palates. Wefts of herbs: sorrels, bedstraws,
mouse ear, hawkbit, eyebright, tormentil, vanishing
flowers: yellow rattle which tells when to cut hay,
slow-growing harebells – dying on verges from nitrous
exhaust, knapweeds, speedwells, trefoils, timothy,
yellow oat grass, sweet vernal grass, all names and niches,
rhizomes and runners, all paraphernalia of panicles, ligules,
shoots, sheaths, spikelets and glumes. All waving grace
and grain – millions of years' resilience to cutting and cropping.
Famine waits as we taint soils, strain genes, skew climate.

To My Miniaturist

Paint me into a circle of sycamores
a bright arena of peeking shades.
I will be standing waiting for tree tops
to still the flitter of small birds.

Craning my neck, I'll tune my ear
to bees nectaring in nearby limes
and share high, sticky, summer
with aphids and ants.

Paint me waiting for a shadow to thunder
into an old, black hound still hunting
galloping to my open arms
not stopping but glancing a nuzzle.

To Enlli

1.
Twenty thousand saints
give way to forty thousand shearwaters
rafting, gliding, skimming –

flipping day to night,
swapping south for north,
north for south,

to stay forever summer.

2.
A pilgrimage not for sainthood,
but for words buoyant as fronds
of bladderwrack cushioning the Cafn,
resilient as the long lines of kelp
crinkling Solfach, for thrift tufts
hackling The Narrows.

A pilgrimage to join the grey seal's
Snort-song, and appraising stare.
For collapsed caves, sky channels
that gurgle smugglers' secrets,
whisper prayers and respond in echoes.

A pilgrimage not for holy relics
but for flotsam, jetsam and spindrift.
For stories taking root at wells,
company in the schoolhouse.
For the constant crossings out
and re-writes of the tide.

Clarach Bay

On the first day,
                    we stirred rock pools,
brushed anemones with grit, teasing them
             to suck and spit
toed the tide-turnings,
               seeking starfish & shells.
We tug-o-warred
               with straps of kelp & bubbled wrack,
rehearsing separation to different schools.

On the second day,
               her eyes scaled the cliff.
My throat gulped dry
            like the gully she chose.

We ratcheted up on dares,
                hard breaths
perilous rests
            the sea a sweeping cloak
that could vanish us – swish
              the way it swallowed Cant're Gwaelod.

She climbed ahead
            dislodged my handhold
and bowled me straight down to vertigo.

In one paralysed grasp
            I knew the heave of rock formation
felt strata buckle.

My limpet powers
                    were weakening
I wished I could soar on a thermal like the choughs.

Stuck – one fixed point
                         in a spinning world.
Giddy. Gravity & gradient ganging up
                              fumble & tumble
D
  O
    W
      N
to the
         S
       H
     I
   N
 G
L
E

Thrust
        to reach tufts of thrift

haul out onto the cliff path
                      and flatline with the far horizon.

Home Bird

What makes your wing trail,
I fear,
is worse than old-age moult.

This sweep as you fan my book for stray seeds
would get you killed
on the other side of the window.

In here, you have my word,
the young hounds who sigh sleepily
at my feet, are on your side.

The primaries
stuck oddly from your white scapula,
sign a kind of angel-dom.

Rain Shadow

So sultry

      you wonder how air can hold

such moisture and not release more

        than a tease –

      a trace on the lip.

A pair of swans at ease on the lake

      beat hard to scale air so heavy.

Brown grasses rasp in the down-draft

Clouds darken and drift off elsewhere.

Theatre of War

Steel shutters fasten village buildings
and shelled houses drop their facades
as swallows sweep shadows from empty attics.

When I woke, I washed my hands in flowing water
And as I stood there,
I saw an eagle fly up to Apollo's altar.

Light drains fast into thin mountain soil
and scant trees sigh after artillery crack.
Rushes hush the chorused lamentations.

Speechless I watched –
and then saw a falcon circling the air,
a hawk, which

in a sudden rush of beating wings
attacked the eagle,
tearing at its crown with vicious talons.

The ghosts of snipers trigger a skim
of house martins flying west.
Peregrine, fleck of the mantling night,

stoops to the hide-out of hazels.
and soars to the apex of the last house
where she feeds her clamourous young.

But the eagle did nothing to protect itself –
It submitted to the onslaught and bloodied wounds,
cowering as its head was ripped asunder.

Below an old army tank rusts and reverberates
iron – metal of blood and bloodshed –
bird cries   stage cries

Before Plastic –

Clues to heaven

lay where oceans washed shores.

Sands inked by sky

a frieze of starfish

& cloud prints

scallop shells fanning sun rays

& whelks whirled from currents

by Earth's spin, Moon's suck.

The far off sense of depths

stilling whale's slumber.

For a Friend Facing Surgery

I send you the dipper, not genuflecting
to the rock but bowing to appetite.
Soon he will submerge and let the river
press him to its bed. He will walk
out again replete to bob and curtsey.

Mother-of-pearl breasted magpies
sip and bathe in pairs, polishing
their black lacquered frames before
swaggering indigo-green sheen
out of the shallows.

On this uncertain day,
swallows soar and flip, stropping
themselves on the clear sky between dark
cloud drifts, showering brilliant blue sparks
down at the dousing river.

A goldfinch flies from silver seeds
illuminating taut power-lines
as an illustrator's gold-leaf motif
heads a new chapter of manuscript
far from marbled endpapers.

Wind through Poplars

On that breathless day, riverside poplars
stirred and sighed.
Heart-sized leaves trembled,
though the wind rested.

I thought it was your voice, whispering, impatient
that my two-year-old legs ran out of strength.
Maybe this was the moment you saw
Mum's illness start in weariness –

foresaw its pain stretching out
like barbed wire – how strands would snap off
and coil around the house, snag us,
no matter how carefully we tried to step through.

As I grew, the poplars called me, their shelter
more generous than the pollarded willows pegging
your childhood territory to mine. Yours bristled
straight along dykes, mine back-bended over meanders.

In the prevailing south-westerlies leaf-speech
is closest to your suppressed hushes
most like the rush of the Kenwater mill race
undercutting roots.

In winter, gnarly trees burl to faces,
mutter like your Low Country German –
groaning over the North Sea
with whispers of old war losses.

On my last visit to you in hospital
I turned my back on TV,
lifted your raspy breaths to the open window
sent them across town

to the same stand of black poplars
which took your restlessness into their own
shushing and hissing
eager to shed their leaves.

Blowing Kisses in Sand

I've always stuck close to the common elements.
The most abundant, my chemistry teacher would say,
not common. That was way back when there were
only ninety-four elements, before we worried about
carbon footprints, and I'd never heard of osteoporosis –
a change to the micro architecture of your bones
- Common frailty. I feel like a splay-legged
glass animal gathering dust on a young girl's shelf.

Chuck in more of the white stuff - more limestone –
I'd say if I was still making glass.
Add calcium to counter brittleness.
And that's the prescription they've given me.
I loved science - all that glass apparatus:
moulded retorts, beakers, basic test-tubes.
I only got to work soft glass but better stuff
than mam's tumblers. One ping of your fingernail

and they'd shatter. I won them for her at the fair.
Not a bad shot even with a cockeyed rifle.
You can see straight son.
Hold things true when they're out of kilter.
Reckon they'd snap you up at the glass works.
That was the closest I got to Big Bang -
no money for me to study astronomy or geology
but I could get paid to play with fire and fuse sands.

Furnace fever - I could keep cool, focus when the beads
of sweat were big as the globs of gather I'd blow.
Keep it glowing by dipping it into the Gloryhole
keep it turning and tilting,
mould it in a mitt of wet newspaper,
fill it with steady out-breaths.
My granddaughter came to watch –
Blow kisses. Blow it with kisses, granddad.

She was my last apprentice.
There aren't many jobs now so she works
weekends showing off in the museum.
I couldn't do it. Haven't got the banter.
But she's like a circus artist, twirling
her blowpipe, juggling the glow, making free
with molten matter. She even lets kids have a go,
see the excitement as it starts, sudden

as a teardrop, then they force it,
want the biggest bubble, as if they're
in a swimming gala and they've got to blow
a glass aqualung. It always shatters -
silver splinters in the floor cracks.
I wouldn't have the patience for such tricks
but I like her take on thermal shock:
the molecules go into nervous breakdown and explode.

I'd flit into the flames if I thought
they'd temper my old bones.

My house is dissolving

Glass wavers to a mirage –
a bumble bee drones through window holes
last slates scatter into swifts.

It was definitely there last night –
I bedded down between barricades of boxes
when the rain began pelting the roof.

It must've decided it isn't needed
since today is cloudless and so blue.
There's just this façade.

Birds drench the hole with song
a small lake gurgles up,
lapping and rippling.

There's nowhere to squat
apart from the tiny proscenium
of the front doorstep.

Inland Gulls

1. *Arrival*

For years it was a few Black-headed gulls
snickering in from Llyn Mawr,

                neat   masked   watchers
                                      stationed on lamp posts
then Common gulls
      drifted in
             always from the north like memories of snow.

Teatimes they squalled the heat haze
                              turning
                      town to a snow-globe

landing raucously in chorus lines at fast food joints

      cruising picnic sites to hustle bins

        and swashbuckle pickings in the river's racing
shallows.

2. *Settling In*

They started staying over
      cwtched up to chimney pots
            ranked themselves on church and cinema roofs.

That summer my student stopped mid-sentence –

Listen! You'd think we were at the seaside, not
the centre of town, wouldn't you?

Flocks cracked into classic keening
                as if mourning their landlocked state
and we Desert Islanded the rest of the lesson
           Maths and Art and History washed around us.

August, they settled at the shopping mall
               copulating by the spinning fins of air-con
keeping us all awake with cries more frivolous than sirens
         more insistent than boy racers' intermittent squeals

and sudden revved up backfirings.

3. *Soap Opera*

Omo   Persil   Daz

I think town gulls are the dreams incarnate of early admen
the ones who boasted they'd add *brightness to whiteness*
battling detergents' white supremacy.

I watch the birds on sports fields, tramping
for worms and staying unspattered, so unlike
my school socks which wicked dirt and washed grey.

They squabble takeaway trays streaked
with gory sauce, wade through gravel
and garbage and they always come up

glittering like the *Tide*   dazzling as *Surf*.

4. *Polymorphs*

There are elements of Everybird in gulls
the soar and stoop of falcons, songbirds'
jab-propulsion, pigeon strut and stage
swagger, waders' slow, reflective preening

echoes of us too   the cries of all our broken
brawling nights   flight patterns scattering
like stray thoughts and suddenly switching to fluent formation.

Timeless gulls:
                    traces of pterodactyl
                                and targeted war drone.

Poppy

Scarlet lady –
ain't the whole truth about me.

Sure, I love red satin & mascara,
making eyes, blowing lipstick kisses

but when the skirts fall
don't you see?

My pod's the model
for a million warheads.

Seeds from my arsenal
last a thousand years

just waiting for the right
kind of disturbance.

Plough me a furrow
gash me a road –

I'll wave to all you drowsy punters
flouncing satins and black lace.

Skimmer

This coat's grown heavy.
Its pockets spit out chips
of quartz and calcite –
too few to lay a trail through darkness,
or forgetfulness of the source.
It isn't this fistful of sparkle
that weighs it down.

Slim and sleek, the perfect skimmer
slips out like a fish seeking water.
Once it would have skipped
rings across the wide river,
ricocheted off the far bank
and come chuckling back
but the river keeps shrinking.

The grayling have gone;
corralled in pools, salmon gasp
for the taste of torrent – a cold charge
to reach clear gravels and spawn.
A cast can't cut trickles.
I linger on shingles tickling out shoals
of flat stones that drop through linings.

A dam is forming round my hem.

Shadows

(i.m. Ballinvalley, an ex-racing greyhound)

Early June
              and already
the trees hold a darkness
                  that can make a black hound vanish.

Times I've stood in whispering shadows
                  calling   calling
for you to thunder

only to have you nuzzle my hand
          as if to say
    don't break the secret of stealth.

Now I track dark paths
          printed with stars of fallen elderflowers
hoping for your breath to mist my hand again.

Cuckoo! Cuckoo!

Wading thigh high through wet grasses
    makes me ten years old again
        chewing and spitting sweet stalks –
                hay meadows were forever.

I know this sward like my classmates' register:
    Buttercup, Campion, Lady's Smock...
           Ragged Robin, Rattle, Sorrel.....
           but it's too quiet – only rain whispers.

Now, the first *Cuckoo* cry cracks open friends' smiles.
        I can't hear it but recall is loud   absence
deafening.   Every spring, Mum and I
        competed to claim the earliest cuckoo.

By May hundreds of heard-but-never-seen cuckoos
calling constantly   close by in the tree,
        close up under the eaves,
drove us to echo, 'Shut-up! Shut-up!'

Decades of slow-fade
                    silent waiting.

A kerfuffle of crows at the boundary hedge –
            a quick-draw of binoculars from holster

At the centre of the mob, misted lenses
            find a grey blur
focus on down-pointed wings as they fly
            leaving a trace of cuckoo on a mind left behind.

Eyes strain for clearer sighting
                    rubbed out lines of old drafts.

Two notes and faraway things come closer.

Walking the Montgomeryshire Canal

I belong with slow moving streams and silty canals.
At ease among weeds, irises, swordy rushes,
I'll crawl under wind-cracked willows, enter alder tunnels'
gnatty darkness and emerge into meadows
where a folded heron glides low over horsetails
and sky that isn't drowned in cloud drops holy blue
on water hatching dragonflies and azure damsels.

I stand aside for small birds to catch flies,
take a wren's ticking off, a blackcap's aria;
watch raven's shadowplay spook a moorhen's steady chug.
After whirligigs' dizzy skating, I steady with the slow-mo
twist of floating snails, hold my breath
for geese that just miss twanging power lines
as they circle a winding hole.

Along a straight stretch thoughts scatter
and return as swallows, ideas are images –
The irregular pulse of a narrow boat's wash
turns to red-finned roach chasing disturbance.
I sing to my hounds but worry a hangnail
remembering when cuckoo flowers echoed
cuckoo calls and curlew cries simmered me from sleep.

Looking for Castell Bryn Amlwg

My finger tip's traced map contours to the site
found kinship with the tight whorl of castle rings
but the rest of me's never visited the stronghold.

Once we glimpsed its motte, sharp-chiselled
by last rays of winter light, but it's elusive –
the metalled road jinks past.

Now, sneaking down the edge of Bryn Shop Wood,
we have the drop on castle earthworks rumpling
back to rabbit terraces and sorrel pasture.

Out in the open, a roaring wind forces the zips
on a falcon's feathers. He hovers resilient to tears
clutching the lines of three counties, two countries –

holding them tight against fighter jet practice.
No need to trespass beyond the old track –
sufficient to see it at this close distance and sense

forced labour, fractures – lives subjugated to stone.
The men conscripted to ditch rock and heave it
into ramparts might look up now and see

an engine the colour of gorse parked in a pit
at the farmstead built with looted stones
and praise the strong arm and jaw of the J.C.B.

Dear Pinsley,

Friend from birth – you echoed my gurgles,
shushed me to sleep flowing between our house
and the railings along the street.

Before racing to town - shucking your history
of feeding monks' fish pools, being a priory drain
and, later, fuelling a mill - you led me on

following through spears of tall rush and wild iris
your pools brought a transfer of heaven I couldn't enter
though sky-coloured dragonflies rose from reflected clouds.

We only fell out when you swallowed my marbles
(some big boys made me roll them on the bridge).
I feared losing you when we moved house

but I could still run down to a new stretch – a stretch
so still, in spring it jellied with spawn, in summer
was amphibious and emerald with duckweed.

I came everyday to discover your teeming depths.
As I grew you took me further afield to meanders
where coiled water-snails let go of milfoil

in a slo-mo sinking to soft silt. Above, your air
was graced by lacewings and mayflies. Trout
leapt, leaving a tease of target ripples.

From my look-out in a cracked-down willow,
I watched over you until diggers came to divert you.
Nine years old, I foolishly trusted you'd survive.

Wimberries

Water beads and berry-bloom are scrying pools.
They show you at your happiest – a girl
on The Long Mynd gathering wimberries

– no thoughts of having me or the pains
that stopped you walking so young.
You're gently combing the low bushes

careful to glean the fruits without bursting them,
O so many berries to make one of granny's pies.
Like me now, you're purple-fingered,

blue-lipped, your tongue chases juice,
prods the elusive fragrance of taste
from these cloud-fed, horizon-coloured fruits.

You gave me this inheritance of glut stains,
my constant harking back to the hills
to cup the wide sky in wild harebells.

Raven at the Ridgeway

Nine years old – our first long car ride
over hills only seen close in family stories
an imagined geography of remote relatives
and rivers, this time: Teme, Mule & Ithon.

Now, at the watershed, this moorland
matches my craving for openness.
Clouds rustle sheep and wild ponies
sun sets them dozing on common land.

Down by Black Gate, a raven lands
on a leaning fence post. Persecuted
almost to mythology then, this bird
holds down the updraft and coraxes.

Silenced by wind and windscreen, I fancy
it said: *You'll live near here one day.*
Pitching north over springs and ditches
it hitched me to the pass and aimed me

over the wide blue swoop of Severn
out to the summits of Aran & Cader.

Notes

Prelude I grew up in Leominster, Herefordshire. The Welsh name for the town is Llanllienni and one translation of its meaning is *Land of Streams*.

Family Flowers Richard Beaumond,1948-2018, composed the *Buttercup Polka*.

Busker was written under the influence of the Cracow Klezmer Band's music *The Prayer*.

They Call Me Red NCB denotes National Coal Board.

Becoming Snowbound D-side wires are distribution wires which go from phones, routers etc to E-side (Exchange side) which connects to the Web network.

On The New Mining Sculpture Erected In Wrexham Town Centre was inspired by a steel sculpture created by Ian Walton, mountaineer and artist, based in North Wales. The sculpture was placed in Wrexham town centre as a guerrilla installation by the artist with help from his rock climbing friends including Evan Kinsey.

At the Pass (Bwlch Glynmynydd) Here is Wikipedia on Dents' gloves: "Dents was established in Worcester in 1777 as a manufacturer of fine leather gloves by John Dent (1751–1811). It is possibly Britain's oldest existing fashion manufacturer.

The Meteorite Hunters was written after visiting The Spaceguard Centre, Powys.

River incident A carnyx was a type of long-necked bronze trumpet used by Iron Age Celts.

Clarach Bay Cantre'r Gwaelod was an area of land which, according to legend, was located in an area west of present-day Wales which is now under the waters of Cardigan Bay.

Theatre of War The author has Kaite O'Reilly's kind permission to quote the words in italics from her award-winning verse-drama *Persians*.

~

For my parents Phyllis & Jack Reynen

~

Acknowledgements

With thanks to: Evan Kinsey, Liz Hinkley, Jan Newton, Nadia Kingsley, Kaite O'Reilly, & Anne Osbourn for reading poem drafts; and to the editors of the following competitions, magazines and e-magazines in which the following poems have appeared:

Frog Schooling & **Silk Roads** in *Maligned Species,* Fair Acre Press.

Black Mountain Chapel in *Cambria.*

Four visits to Mitchell's Fold 2 & 3 in *We're All In This Together,* Offa's Press; and *The Poetry of Shropshire,* Offa's Press.

Busker, For a Friend Facing Surgery, Skimmer, & Wimberries in *Muddy Fox,* Rack Press. *Skimmer* also in *Planet.*

A charm of goldfinches in *Beyond Spring - Wanderings through Nature* by Matthew Oates, Fair Acre Press.

February on Reservoir Hill in *Creative Countryside.*

Confession & Working Museum, in *Wolf Hoard - a Border Poets' Anthology.*

They call Me Red in *Encounters* poetry-art exhibition, Shrewsbury. Based on an image by Bob Charlesworth.

At Newbridge-on-Wye School in *Envoi.*

The Meteorite Hunters in The British Council and Sampad's anthology *Inspired by my Museum.*

First Aid selected by Gwyneth Lewis to be displayed on a Guernsey bus.

Yews in a Welsh Border Churchyard won the *Thomas Gray Society Tercentenary Prize*, 2016, judged by Dalgit Nagra.

Another Church Tour selected by David Tait for *The Poetry School* website.

To Enlli in *The Stony Thursday Book,* Limerick Arts.

Blowing Kisses in Sand in *The Poetry of the Black Country,* Offa's Press. It was also commended by John Hartley Williams in the *Keats Shelley Poetry Prize.*

Inland Gulls in *Diversifly - poetry and art on the Urban Birds of Britain*, Fair Acre Press.

Poppy in *Dreamcatcher.*

Cuckoo! Cuckoo! in *The 2017 R.S. Thomas Festival Anthology*, selected by Gillian Clarke & Ifor Ap Glyn.

Walking the Montgomery Canal in *Agenda Online Supplement 13.*

Dear Pinsley, in The Writers' Cafe Magazine.

Raven at the Ridgeway, as Raven at the Watershed, on the *Ledbury Poetry Festival* website: poetry-festival.co.uk/the-malvern-hills/